DREAMLAND

5

I WANT TO KNOW ABOUT

HOW WERE THE FIRST CARS LIKE ?

and other questions about inventions

Compiled by :
Meesha Khanna

Illustrated by :
Kiran & Mohan

D1529511

Published by

DREAMLAND PUBLICATIONS

J-128, KIRTI NAGAR, NEW DELHI - 110 015 (INDIA)
Tel : 011-2510 6050 Fax : 011-2543 8283
E-mail : dreamland@vsnl.com
www.dreamlandpublications.com

Published in 2008 by
DREAMLAND PUBLICATIONS
J-128, Kirti Nagar, New Delhi - 110 015 (India)
Tel : 011-2510 6050, Fax : 011-2543 8283
E-mail : dreamland@vsnl.com, www.dreamlandpublications.com

Copyright © 2008 Dreamland Publications
All rights reserved. No part of this publication should be
reproduced, stored in a retrieval system or transmitted in any
form or by any means—electronic, mechanical, photocopying,
recording or otherwise—without the prior permission of
Dreamland Publications.

ISBN 978-81-8451-033-1

Printed by

EIH LIMITED

A member of The Oberoi Group
UNIT PRINTING PRESS

PREFACE

'I Want To Know About' series provides young children with an excellent starting-point for exploring different topics. It is designed to capture the imagination of the children and arouse their curiosity to know more about many fascinating facts. It is a fun-filled, entertaining book. It also answers demanding questions in a child-friendly and informative style.

The entire series is the result of well-integrated efforts of the entire team of Dreamland. It is hoped that the intended purpose of this book meets the children's requirement.

—Publisher

CONTENTS

Do you know why people invent things ?

People invent things to create answer for their problems. Inventors think about the requirements of people and also how they can make things easy for them. The folding umbrella was invented when it was noticed that big umbrellas were inconvenient.

● Today the life has become very easy with so many inventions around us. Tube lights, pillows and even cornflakes all have made our lives easy and comfortable.

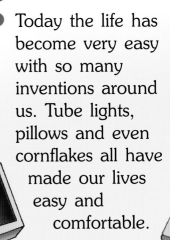

● When someone prepared a glue that didn't stick correctly, post-it notes were invented. You could glue down a piece of paper, pul it off and then re-stick it.

● Do you know that the first Frisbee was invented by a baker named Joseph Frisbee. This idea was born in his mind when he saw some of his customers threw the empty pie tins to each other in the park.

● Burdock seeds are covered with small hooks that attach to things, but can be drawn off. An engineer who saw this used his discovery to build Velcro for fastenings.

- The invention of safety pins took place almost 200 years ago, but they have a long history. The person who invented it copied the thought from clasps worn by the Ancient Egyptians.

Do you know some things are not invented only discovered ?

Coal and rubber were not invented, they were only discovered. An invention is something new which never existed before. For example, a paper-clip.

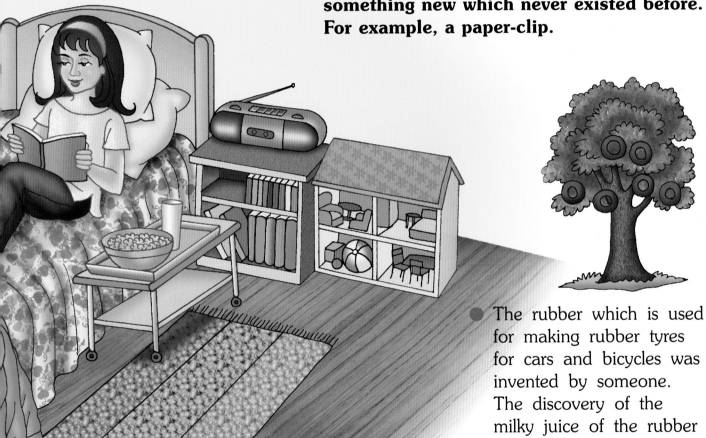

- The rubber which is used for making rubber tyres for cars and bicycles was invented by someone. The discovery of the milky juice of the rubber tree made it possible.

From where do inventors get ideas of invention ?

There are several places from where inventors get ideas for their inventions. A few of them study plants and animals to observe how they have worked out with their problems. Others look at ideas from other places or from the past. Very few ideas come out of the blue.

Do you know how was lipstick invented?

The first lipstick was a smooth colour crayon inside a case that could be wound up and used in a second. American scientists in 1915, invented it. It was a great achievement.

● Ancient Egyptian women used golden clayay mixed with juicy tree sap. This was because they didn't have wind-up lipsticks.

How were false teeth made?

About 2,500 years back people started to make artificial teeth from ivory or bone. Hippo bone was well-liked, but so was ox, cat and human bone. Unluckily, all these artificial teeth quickly turned brown and started to decay. They must have tasted terrible. !

- Lip colours came in a pot, before the invention of a lipstick. Most of the lip colours were waxes and ointments coloured with plant dyes such as grape juice.

- To show the clients how they would look like, a French hairdresser used a video camera linked to a computer. The computer showed the face with short hair, long hair, or with no hair at all ?

Who invented the first plaster ?

Earl Dickson's wife kept cutting herself in the kitchen. So he fixed small squares of cloth on to pieces of sticky tape, covering them cautiously to prevent the glue from drying out. Every time his wife cut herself, she just grasped a part of the tape, and stuck it on. In this way, the first plaster was invented.

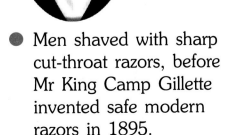

- Men shaved with sharp cut-throat razors, before Mr King Camp Gillette invented safe modern razors in 1895.

Who built the first flushing toilet?

Sir John Harrington built the first flushing toilet for his godmother, Queen Elizabeth I, four hundred years ago. As in those days very few homes had water pipes or drains, so common people had to carry on using their chamber pots.

- About 100 years back, flush toilets were often beautifully decorated with fruits, flowers, animals or shells. As they were highly-prized pieces of furniture.

- The trouble with this shower from the 1800s was that you had to pump the water yourself by foot. By no means had it really jammed !

Who enjoyed the first bath ?

The people of Greece, Rome and the Indus Valley in Pakistan first jumped in the bath in ancient times. But, as the time passed, people stopped bathing. Instead of bathing, they started using perfumes.

● The first toothbrushes were made by the Chinese from the pig's hair. Luckily, in 1930s nylon brushes were made.

How did the first carpet-cleaning machine work ?

The first carpet-cleaning machine was pulled by horses ! It was parked outside the house because of its smelly petrol engine. Long pipes extended through the windows and sucked up all the dust. It was fairly a view and people frequently encouraged their friends around to look at !

Do you know who invented raincoats ?

Raincoats were invented by Charies Macintosh in 1823. For this reason they are often called macs. He sandwiched a layer of rubber between two lengths of cotton and made the cloth waterproof. The coats kept public dry, but they weighed a ton and stink dreadfully when they got wet !

● The hill farmers buy raincoat for their sheep as it rains a lot in Scotland.

How do Zips open or close ?

Zips can not open or close without their teeth. The two rows of teeth are attached by a slide, which locks them together or pulls them separately. In the 1890s, zips were invented and were a huge development on complex buttons and hooks and eyes.

● PVC is a plastic-backed material out of which a lot of today's rainwear is made. It comes in lots of bright colours.

● Levi Strauss made first denim jeans for gold miners in the USA. He used a hard-wearing blue cloth that was used to make tents.

Are clothes also good for health ?

Some clothes are full of health-giving vitamins, which are usually only found in fresh fruits and vegetables !

● In 1820, when Thomas Hancock invented elastic, he considered that it would be helpful along the top of pockets to prevent thieves. It was someone else who understood it would be just correct for holding up people's underwear !

When were electric fridges invented?

Around 1920, electric fridges were invented. Before then icebox was used by the people to keep their food. Huge blocks from the iceman kept the icebox cold.

● John Pemberton invented a sweet syrup in 1885 named Coca-Cola. At that time it was a fizzy drink. Soda water was added to it later.

● For the delivery of large blocks of ice for the ice box, the ice man was called several times in a week.

Do you know who invented the cornflakes?

The invention of cornflakes was an accident. When the two brothers Will and John Kellogg were trying to make a new type of bread, they over cooked a pan of wheat, rolled the mixture flat and then watched it dry into flakes. After toasting the flakes, they tasted them. It was delicious.

Long time back, in winter's, people made natural fridges by lining caves and holes with a thick layer of snow.

The first potato crisps were invented in 1853, when a diner asked from a chef for an extra-thin chips.

Who invented the first drinking straw ?

A man named Marvin Stone made the first paper straw in 1880s. This invention took place when he saw that people kept drinks cooler by not touching the glass and using a hollow grass stalk for drinking the liquid.

Who was called Teddy?

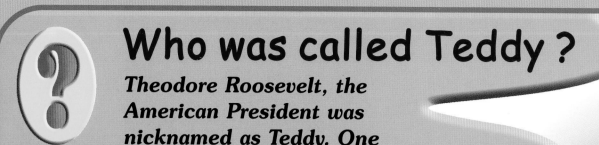

Theodore Roosevelt, the American President was nicknamed as Teddy. One day, he went on a hunting trip and came across a bear cub but refused to shoot it. On reading this story from the newspaper, a sweetshop owner decided to give up his shop and make toy bears. He named them Teddy Bear, after the President.

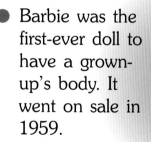

● Barbie was the first-ever doll to have a grown-up's body. It went on sale in 1959.

How oldest are the dolls?

Dolls are 6,000 years old and most likely the oldest toys of all. Dolls have been prepared from all kinds of materials-wood, wax, paper, china and plastic. Roman children played with dolls made of rags.

Do you know when home computer games appear ?

In 1974, the first home computer games appeared. They were not very exciting as compared to today's games. In outer space there were no life-and-death battles.

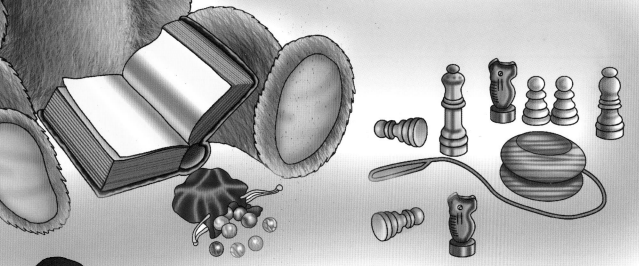

● The building toys Meccano and Lego were both invented to persuade children to construct things, not demolish them to create all sorts of inventions !

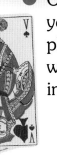

● Over 1,000 years ago, playing cards were invented in Asia.

When was the first pop-up toaster invented?

The first pop-up toaster was invented in the USA about 70 years ago. Before the invention of electric toasters, people used to put a piece of bread on the end of a long toasting fork, and held it in front of a fire. But this was not a very easy task. As the bread burnt easily and needed very careful watching.

● Electric toasters are very helpful, as they save the toasts from burning.

● An automatic tea - making machine was invented in 1937. In the beginning it was named as the Cheerywake, but soon the name was changed to the Teasmade. It heated water, made the tea and then an alarm used to ring.

How was the microwave oven invented?

Just after the second world war Percy Spencer invented the microwave oven. To detect enemy planes, he had been working on ways of using invisible waves. He realized that the waves are useful for cooking too, when they melted the chocolate bar in his pocket.

● Microwaves are a form of electromagnetic wave. It takes energy to produce light, whether it comes from the sun, a kerosene lamp or a light blub. Microwaves are used to generate heat which passes through the food and cooks it quickly.

● Only rich people used to afford electricity in their homes, about 100 years ago. Servants sometimes risked their lives by using the first electrical gadgets, as they were dangerous things.

When was Teflon invented ?

Teflon was invented in late 1930. It is a kind of plastic which is as slippery as ice. Due to this reason, non-stick pans don't stick, as they are coated with Teflon. But after many years this idea came to someone's mind.

4 LAYER INTERLOCKING NONSTICK COATING

INTERIOR SURFACE

EXTERIOR SURFACE

Who invented the basketball ?

About 100 years ago, James Naismith invented the basketball. He was looking for an exciting game to play indoors on cold winter nights. The very first basketball players used two old peach basket as goals.

● Things are easier today, for the basketball players. Earlier they had to climb a ladder to get the ball back after a goal. But now the goal nets have a hole in the bottom.

What makes trainers so springy ?

The springy soles made of rubber and little pockets of air make the trainers so springy. Every time you take a step, the rubber gets compressed down, but rapidly leaps back to its original size. All this squashing and springing makes your feet bounce off the ground, and help you to run more rapidly.

● In the late 1800s roller-skating became a passion. In Paris, ballerinas even danced at the ballet in them !

How were roller skates invented ?

Before the invention of the roller skates, there were ice rinks. People could only ice-skate outdoors in the winter. Then someone came up with the thought of making a 'ground' skate that people could enjoy in the summer, too. Instead of a blade, they put wheels on the sole and the roller skates were invented !

● In Japan, in 1979, Jet-skis first went on sale. Jet-skiers have to steer well clear of bathers. Most recent models can go fast at speeds of 105 km/h.

How were the first cars like ?

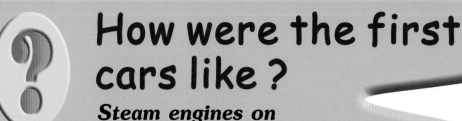

Steam engines on wheels were the first cars. But they used to scare other road users as they were noisy smoky machines. They were, used for nearly 30 years, as they were more quicker and easier to drive. They were replaced by faster cars with petrol engines.

● The speed of the first cars were limited to 3km/h. To warn other road users, someone had to walk in front with a flag !

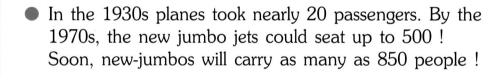

● In the 1930s planes took nearly 20 passengers. By the 1970s, the new jumbo jets could seat up to 500 ! Soon, new-jumbos will carry as many as 850 people !

Who invented the hovercraft ?

In 1959, Christopher Cockerell invented the hovercraft. He discovered that trapping a cushion of air under a boat raises it up above the waves, permitting it to travel much quicker.

● Everybody knows about seat belts for people to wear, but did you know that cats and dogs can wear them too ?

● In 1860s the penny-farthing bicycle was invented. It was named after two British coins of the time-the large penny and the tiny farthing. This was because it had two wheels-one very large and one very small.

Do bikes have sails ?

The fastest superbikes have firm wheels and flat frames that work in the similar way as a sail. As the bike zooms along, its wheels and frame grasp the wind, which helps to push the bike forward just as it does on a boat. But most of the control still comes from turning the pedals !

How are CD-ROMs helpful?

There's space for about 1,000 storybooks on a CD-ROM a small compact disc that's as thin as your fingernail and can adjust in a pocket. Words, pictures and sounds can all be accumulated on CD-ROMs, but they only work with a computer so you cannot study one on the bus—yet !

● One of the first people to write with ink were the Egyptians. They prepared it by mixing sticky tree sap with black soot.

● Typewriter was invented in 1873. But now it has been replaced by computers and word-processors. So it will soon be extinct, just like dinosaurs.

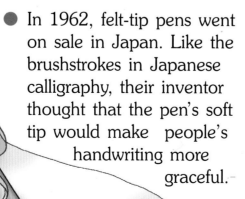

● In 1962, felt-tip pens went on sale in Japan. Like the brushstrokes in Japanese calligraphy, their inventor thought that the pen's soft tip would make people's handwriting more graceful.

Which was the first computer?

The first computer was built in Britain and was switched on in 1943. It was named as Colossus and was about as long as four buses.

● Today's pocket calculators can bear out calculations much faster than you can move your fingers. They are as powerful as the giant computers of the 1960s.

Who invented the ballpoint pen?

In 1938, Ladislao Biro invented the ballpoint pen. It included a tube of long-term, quick-drying ink, which moved evenly onto the paper with a tiny ball at the tip. Even though Biro called his pen a ball-point, a good number of people now call their ballpoint a biro !

How was a cash register invented?

James Ritty, who had a saloon in Ohio, USA invented a cash register in 1879. This invention came in his mind when he saw that customers were always arguing with the staff about how much they had to pay for their rinks. Ritty's register rang up the prices, kept a record of how much money was in the till and gave Ritty and his staff a much more peaceful life.

What happened before the invention of coins?

Before the invention of coins, people used to swap things like shells, beads or grain for the goods they wanted. People in Tibet and China once used tea pressed into blocks as money.

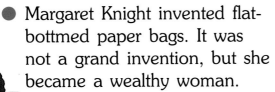

● Margaret Knight invented flat-bottmed paper bags. It was not a grand invention, but she became a wealthy woman. These bags could carry twice as much shopping !

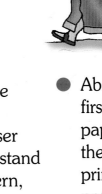

● About 1200 years ago, first people to use the paper bank-notes were the Chinese. They printed some of their notes on the bank of the mulberry tree.

● Goods sold in shops have had a bar code on them since 1980. Only a laser scanner can understand the bar code's pattern, which contains all sorts of information about the item.

Who invented a supermarket trolley?

Sylvan Glodman was the person who invented the world's first supermarket trolley. It was little more than a chair on wheels, with two baskets attached on the top, but it earned him a fortune.

What appeared first-screws or screwdrivers?

Spiral or twisted nails were used in the 1500s in guns, armour and clocks. But, oddly, you could not unscrew a screw for another 300 years when the handy screwdriver first came.

● Today also many carpenters use the same tools which were used by the carpenters long back.

● Till 1760s, screws were not made by machine. The thread that surrounds the screw had to be filed by hand. That must have been a difficult task.

Who invented lock and key?

Locks were invented by Ancient Egyptians. Two wooden bolts were fixed together tightly and were held in place by pins set in a pattern. The pins could only be fixed with a key which had an identical pattern.

Who pulled the first lawnmowers?

Horses pulled the first lawnmowers. The animals had to wear big rubber boots so, they didn't leave untidy hoof-prints all over the freshly mown lawn !

- Even if you do not have a garden you can grow plants anywhere with Gro-bags. In 1973, these big bags of earth first appeared.

- Lawnmower engines were used on the first go-karts. Today's Grand Prix Champions possibly all started out driving lawnmowers !

Who took the first-ever photograph ?

In 1826, a Frenchman named Joseph Niepce took the first-ever photograph. But it took hours to take one picture. As he had to wait eight hours before the picture was captured on a thin metal plate coated with a sort of tar.

View Through a Window at Grasse, 1826.

● The fact that today's Polaroid cameras can produce a picture in seconds, Niepce would not have believed it !

● It took so long to take a photo in the late 1800s, that sitters needed a back-rest to help them sit still !

Who invented the pink TV ?

John Logie Baird invented the first TV which had an odd picture-bright pink and very fuzzy ! He used a very odd equipment to build it, including a bicycle light and a knitting needle.

When was the personal stereo invented?

The personal stereo was invented in 1979 by a Japanese electrical company named Sony. A personal cassette player, also known as a walkman also had headphones with it. It is light enough to carry around.

- The size of the world's smallest radio is equal to about the size of a pea !

- In 1878, in a small town in the USA, the first telephone service started. Only 20 people would ring up each other as only they had phones.

What is a virtual reality helmet?

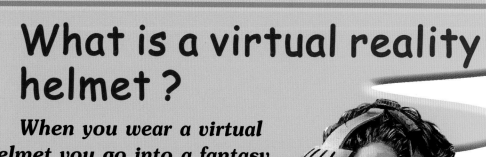

When you wear a virtual reality helmet you go into a fantasy world. You could be struggling with a man-eating dinosaur or visiting aliens in space. Everything within the helmet looks and sounds real, but is in fact created by a computer.

● The computer changes the pictures you see and the sounds you hear, as you press buttons in the special data-glove.

● You could also be an inventor, if you wish to invent something.

Do Mars also have insects?

Till now there are no insects on the Mars. But, scientists are constructing small robots to discover Mars and other planets. The robots have six legs and look somewhat like huge insects. They appear to act like insects too, because they have been programmed to search for food. The food is not for them, though it is for us, if we ever live on Mars !

● In the future cars may have a computer on board, which could prepare the drivers route. It would even warn drivers of obstructions on the road ahead advice a good short-cut.

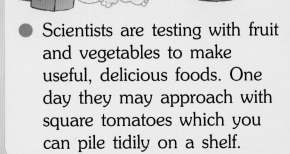

● Scientists are testing with fruit and vegetables to make useful, delicious foods. One day they may approach with square tomatoes which you can pile tidily on a shelf.

Index